Dragonfly Dreams

A mother's dream for her children

Written and Illustrated by

Kathryn Anderson

www.KathrynAndersonbooks.com

Cover and Illustrations by

Rhonda Daigler

Balboa Press books may be ordered through booksellers or by contacting:

Balboa Press
A Division of Hay House
1663 Liberty Drive
Bloomington, IN 47403
www.balboapress.com
844-682-1282

ISBN: 978-1-9822-7136-7 (sc)
978-1-9822-7137-4 (e)

Library of Congress Control Number: 2021914077

Print information available on the last page.

Balboa Press rev. date: 07/15/2021

BALBOA.PRESS
A DIVISION OF HAY HOUSE

Dedication

This book is dedicated to my son's Jonathon and Joshua....
To be your mother is my greatest honor... I Love you both forever and always....
and of course my grandaughter Quinny!

Love

Mom

A dragonfly said to his mother,
"I'm afraid to fly, what if I fail."

The mother dragonfly with a tear in her eye
pushed the little dragonfly out and said,
"My Love, what if you fly,
your dragonfly dream is very close by."

Momma said to her sweet brand new son,
who was crying mightily as his life begun,
"Hush my child you are safe and loved….
Oh welcome my precious gift from above."

The baby cried thinking *what if I fail*.

The Momma with tears of happiness
cried and nestled him in, right by her side.
"What if you fly and trust in
the Lord all of your life?"

The Momma said to her
sweet one-year-old son,
"You can walk now if you try,
I'll catch you if you take a baby nose dive."

The baby thought *what if I fail….*
The mother thought *what if you fly (walk)*

"Trust in the Lord and you will be alright."

The toddler was trying to ride his bike
to peddle and peddle with all of his might.

The boy screamed out, "What if I fail…."

The mother sung out,
"But what if you fly, ride my boy, ride
and trust God by your side."

The five-year old boy was starting school
standing at the bus stop,
he let out a gulp and a drool.

His first day of school
the little boy was afraid…
The Momma hugged him gently and said,
"Everything will be OK."

The boy said in a little sob,
"But what if I fail and no one likes me at all?"

"Oh my sweet, sweet boy,
what if you fly and gather new friends…
Trust in the Lord on him you can depend."

Now the boy is thirteen,
a boy scout with a lot of dreams.

The night of the survival weekend
the boy said to his mother,
"What if I fail and don't get my badge?"

The mother said loudly,
while waving goodbye…
"My boy scout will become
an eagle and what if you fly."

"I trust in God; He is right by your side."

The boy is now sixteen years old,
with very strange friends
and his eye on a girl he wanted to know.

The boy while funny and goofy with
his friends was timid by this girl…
Would she like him in the end?

The boy was thinking, *"What if I fail…"*

The Momma thinking what if you fly, I trust
in God to have the right girl by your side…

The boy is now a college grad...
Afraid to go forward, what job should he have?

The boy told his mother I am scared to fail,
"What if I don't like this job either,
my life with derail?"

The mother then answered, "Oh my sweet son,
the knowledge you are gathering has just begun."

"But Mom what if I don't like it and fail?"

"Oh my son what if you find your
passion on your journey and fly...
You can do this with God as your guide."

The boy is now a young man with a
beautiful wife and a baby on hand.
"What if I'm not a good father, what if I fail?"

The mother smiled back, "Oh my sweet son,
look to God to get the job done...
The Love you have is great my dear,
point them up and do not fear."

"But Mom what if I fail?"

"My handsome son, what if you fly...
Your children are blessed to
have you by their side...
God has got you, find your strength in him...
You just have to ask to let it begin."

Long, long down the road….

The mother said, "I am growing old,
I do not have much time.
My dragonfly dreams for you my child
is to fly on God's wings and
don't stop but smile.

This earthly world is but a blip,
so enjoy and leave your signature
of God's Love on it."

The son looked at his mother
as she took her last breath and
in a very low voice he said,
"Mom, I'm afraid."

She grabbed his hand with
a tear in her eye and said softly,
"I love you my son, it's your time to fly.

"I'm going back home but this is not goodbye…
Your Dragonfly dream is now very close by…

"I'm with you always in all you do,
just count on God he'll see you through…

"For it's the Love you take with you
when you go back home…

"I'm with you always, your life is my poem."

Love forever,
Mom

"God said, come to me as children.
So I've written children's books for adults, too."
- Kathy Anderson

Children's book author and illustrator,
Kathryn Anderson lives in a small town in New York with her family.
She loves to teach and inspire children to let them know
that they are loved and valued through her stories.
Kathy's other books can be found on Amazon
www.kathrynanderson15.wixsite.com/inspirechildbooks

Little Lottie and the Lying Octopus
Mean Green Grouchy Larry
How Ansley Brynn Got Her Wings
My Child You Are Safe
Steve the Big Nose Monkey
A Soldier Story
Friends
Angels and Butterflies

Rhonda Daigler the primary illustrator, lives in Pendleton,
New York with her family.
She is the owner of Artisan Alley where she loves teaching art to all ages.
You can find her beautiful art work at
www.lazycreekart.com

LOVE

My Family

Thank you to my beautiful family;
my husband Steve, My son Jon and beautiful
daughter-in-law Erin, my son Josh and my inquisitive,
gorgeous granddaughter Quinny...
I Love you all forever!

the boy and his mom

Printed in the United States
by Baker & Taylor Publisher Services